750 Ways
to
Annoy People

W. Shaffer Fox

Cosmic Mind
B O O K S

Published by: **Cosmic Mind Books**

All rights reserved. No part of this book may be reproduced or transmitted in any form or by any means, electronic or mechanical, including photocopying, recording or by any information storage and retrieval system without written permission from the author, except for the inclusion of brief quotations in professional articles or reviews. For more information, contact: **Cosmic Mind Books, P. O. Box 150048, Arlington, TX 76015 U. S. A.**

All names of persons and other entities listed in or on this book, other than the names of the publisher, the author, the graphic artist, those listed on this page and trade names, are fictitious and their similarities to persons/entities past or present, living or deceased, are purely coincidental.

Copyright © 1999 by W. Shaffer Fox
First printing: 1999

Library of Congress Catalog Card Number: 99-64035
Title: 750 Ways to Annoy People
Author: W. Shaffer Fox

ISBN 0-9672399-9-0

Printed in the United States of America. Printed on acid-free paper.
Cover by Cosmic Mind Books & Louis Iglesias. Cover illustrations & graphics by Louis Iglesias.

Introduction

Several people have written books describing w[hat] *bothers* them, what *disturbs* them, what *irritates* them, w[hat] *upsets* them, what *aggravates* them, what *pisses-them-off*; what causes them *pain, anger, distress, bitterness, agony, embarrassment, grief, depression, disgust, anxiety, sorrow, mortification,* etcetera, etcetera, on and on, ad infinitum, ad nauseam!

Enough already!

It's time for you to quit whining and to quit being a victim. It's time for you to switch from being reactive to being proactive. It's time for you to become the aggressor. It's time for you to become that stellar purveyor of mayhem who floats through life reeking emotional havoc upon all with whom you come in contact. *750 Ways to Annoy People* shows you how to do just that. Implementing the actions listed in *750 Ways to Annoy People* will cause those who are dignified to decompose before your very eyes. It can also earn for you the esteemed moniker: "That Freaking Weirdo!"

Yes, you, too, can become the person who even psychiatrists want to avoid, and S. W. A. T. officers dream about attacking.

Warning — Disclaimer

But, of course, we do not want you to do, and you MUST NOT do, any of the ridiculous things listed in this book. The sole purpose of this book is to entertain the reader. After all, hey, this is just a humor book!

The author and/or Cosmic Mind Books shall have neither liability nor responsibility to any person or entity with respect to any loss or damage caused, or alleged to be caused, directly or indirectly by the information contained in this book. If you do not wish to be bound by the above, listed under Warning — Disclaimer, return the book along with the sales receipt to the publisher for a full refund, and don't read beyond this page. Either way, we wish you well.

750 Ways
to
Annoy People

1.   Marry the boss's son or daughter.

2.   Drive around lost for hours rather than stopping to ask for directions.

3.   When bowling, take your shots overhand.

4.   Write with green, orange, pink or purple ink.

5.   Fail to keep promises.

6.   Eat with your mouth open.

7.   Tuck your napkin into your shirt collar.

8.   Place "out of order" signs on working vending machines.

9.   When talking with a police officer, refer to him or her as "General."

10.   Completely cut up your entire meal before you begin eating it.

11.   Put 25 watt light bulbs in all light sockets.

12.   Brag.

13. Be lazy.

14. Ask for refunds.

15. Talk out loud in libraries.

16. Yell at the people on your television set.

17. Make scary faces at babies.

18. Leave your turn signal on without changing lanes or turning.

19. Adjust your car's headlight beams so that they are shooting off in different, weird directions.

20. Wear your pants pulled up high above your waist.

21. Let others pay the check.

22. When you get into an elevator, press all the buttons.

23. When you shake hands with a person, tickle their palm with your index finger.

24.   Fidget.

25.   Laugh for no reason.

26.   Put Monopoly money in the collection plate at church.

27.   Don't brush your teeth for a week before going to the dentist.

28.   Finish people's sentences for them.

29.   On every letter always add a "P. S.," then a "P. S. S.," then a P. S. S. S," then a P. S. S. S. S....."

30.   Change your name, and then proclaim that your new name is actually your original name from a past life.

31.   Wear colored underwear that shows through your clothes.

32.   If you're a man, start wearing makeup.

33.   Sometimes answer your phone by saying, "EeeeeYel-low," and other times by screaming, "WHAT THE HELL DO YOU WANT?"

34.   Leave the door open when you use the bathroom.

35. Telephone radio talk shows and keep talking and talking and talking until they hang up on you.

36. Address envelopes upside down.

37. Carve notches into the edges of rulers.

38. Move into a house trailer.

39. Put gaudy, fuzzy covers on your toilet seats and tanks.

40. Call the police every day and yell at them: "Okay. Here we go again.

There was another flying saucer here last night. Now when are you idiots going to do something about this problem?"

41. Cut in front of people.

42. Cancel your garbage service.

43. Wear dark colored socks with sandals and shorts.

44. At the end of a first date, get angry and say: "You don't have any intentions of marrying me, do you?"

45.   Drive on the shoulders of roads.

46.   Become a militant female minister, mullah, priest or rabbi.

47.   Vigorously brush your hair at the dinner table. Tell people that you might not have time to do it again before you go to bed.

48.   In the fall, rake your leaves onto your neighbor's lawn.

49.   Bang pots and pans, vacuum, and leave the television blasting in the background while you're on the phone.

50.   Get vanity license plates for your car.

51.   Wear a white belt and white shoes.

52.   Walk up to strangers, male or female, and kiss them on the lips while simultaneously inserting your tongue and frenching wildly.

53.   Decorate your television set with flowers, pictures and tacky, irrelevant nicknacks.

54.   Interrupt people.

55.   Never admit that you are wrong.

56.   Whine intermittently.

57.   Bite your fingernails.

58.   Squirt glue into the keyholes of locks.

59.   Grow a great, big protruding butt, and waddle when you walk.

60.   When the wine steward at a fine restaurant offers you a sample, taste it, then spit it all over him and scream: "How dare you try to pawn-off

this swill on *me* — of all people. I'm a licensed security guard!

61.   Use a different color of polish on each of your fingernails.

62.   Suck on your teeth.

63.   Wear dress shirts buttoned to the collar without a tie.

64.   End every statement by exclaiming: "So sayeth the Lord!"

65.   Roll your own cigarettes.

66.   Claim that you have degrees from elite universities.

67.   Put food and fabric dyes into liquid soap dispensers.

68.   Get a nose job.

69.   Drive at night with just your parking lights on.

70.   Tint your car windows black.

71.   Pull a rotted wood, trash-filled, homemade trailer — that weaves all over the road — behind your car.

72.   Don't make eye contact with people.

73.   Constantly jingle the change in your pocket(s).

74.   Fail to be available when you are really needed.

75.   Decorate with velvet paintings.

76.   Have a limp handshake.

77.   Lick your fingers while you are eating.

78.   Develop an acquired, upper class accent. Save it for when you really want to make a point.

79.   Marry a much younger woman or a much younger man.

80.   Call home improvement companies after hours and leave the following message: "Yes, I need to have the exterior of my 32,000 square foot summer home sided immediately. I'm elderly, I'm blind, I have no family, and I'm rich and I'll pay cash. Please call me right away." Then leave a fictitious name and an incomplete phone number.

81.   Drink milk directly from the carton.

82. Punch pin holes in the bottoms of other people's milk cartons.

83. Install flood lights in your yard which shine into your neighbor's windows.

84. Loudly whistle entire songs.

85. Tell house guests that your home is haunted by evil spirits.

86. Grow a mustache on only one side of your lip.

87. During every telephone conversation state: "By the way, I should

inform you that I am recording this call."

88.   If you are a man, begin referring to yourself as a prince, and if you're a woman, begin referring to yourself as a princess. For example, "Hello, this is Prince Thomas calling...," or, "Hello, this is Princess Carol calling...." If people ask what you are a prince or princess of, say: "It's none of your earwax, stupid!"

89.   Claim that you were the true hero of every important event.

90.   Eat dessert before the first course.

91.   Tell everyone that you have a twelve inch "man o' war."

92.   Drive around your neighborhood squealing your tires, lighting fire-crackers and honking your horn at 4:00 a.m.

93.   Grow a vegetable garden in your front yard.

94.   Cheat at any game you are playing — then deny it.

95.   Get an extremely tight-curl permanent.

96.   Proclaim that an obscure gambling casino/tavern, somewhere in rural

Nevada, is the classiest place on earth.

97.   Plug multiple electrical devices into a single receptacle.

98.   Name your child after an ex-lover.

99.   Ask people which sign they are.

100.   Wear turquoise jewelry.

101.   Smack unsuspecting people in the head with a rolled-up newspaper. Tell them that you are trying to kill pigeons for tomorrow's brunch.

102.   Shortly after arriving at any party, walk up to the host and say: "I'm leaving. This party sucks!"

103.   Don't flush toilets after use.

104.   Wear too much makeup.

105.   Sniff instead of blowing your nose.

106.   Claim that your age is younger than it actually is.

107.   Put a "Do Not Disturb" sign on your desk.

108. Circumvent chains of command.

109. Ask your chiropractor if he or she is an M. D.

110. Use people.

111. Insist that your mate prepare for sex by getting dressed up like a circus clown.

112. Drive the wrong way on one-way streets.

113. Complain constantly.

114.   Include the term "you know" in every sentence.

115.   Put more than two scoops of sugar into your coffee or tea.

116.   If you have an associate's degree, always make sure to note it after your name. For example: Stewart Jones, A. S.
                                                  1015 East Main St.
                                                  Flatonia, WI   556655

117.   Read other people's diaries.

118.   Holler random numbers at people who are counting.

119.   Invite friends over for a late dinner party. After they have arrived and gotten comfortable, tell them that you couldn't afford to buy any food.

120.   Ask people what gender they are.

121.   Whenever you are playing a game, vehemently accuse others of cheating.

122.   Wear a full-cover ski mask 24-hours per day.

123.   Claim that you hold patents on things you obviously didn't invent.

124. Put several "My child's an honor student at...." bumper stickers on your car.

125. Call people who are fat "Skinny." Call people who are skinny "Fatso."

126. Keep the door to your office locked at all times. After a few months, install a doorbell.

127. Control your children by putting them on leashes.

128. Refuse to learn how to use a computer.

129.   Remove toilet paper from restrooms.

130.   Stand in your front yard pointing a hair dryer at passing cars.

131.   Take a baby to a movie.

132.   Add additional initials to your name. For example: "Hello, this is W. A. K. J. T. L. V. M. F. Smith calling...."

133.   Have a coughing fit at a salad bar.

134.   Touch the food at a salad bar with your fingers.

135.   Pick up food at a salad bar, taste it, then put it back.

136.   Stack used dirty dishes on the table.

137.   Read while you are driving.

138.   Claim that you only watch P. B. S. on television.

139.   Spit.

140.   Crack your knuckles.

141.   Staple papers in the middle of the page.

142.   Talk about yourself in the third person.

143.   Cut yourself shaving and leave the house with bits of bloody toilet paper stuck all over your face and neck.

144.   When other drivers try to pass you — speed up.

145.   Buy a cheap paperback about King Tut and, thereafter, lecture as though you are a credentialed Egyptologist.

146.   Put paprika on mashed potatoes and then rave about the presentation.

147.   To save a few bucks on motels during your vacations, finance a huge, unwieldy, $70,000.00, quickly depreciating R. V.

148.   Park the R. V. in your driveway.

149.   Wear your high school class ring beyond high school.

150.   Tell everyone at your health club that you have the worst case of athlete's foot you've ever seen.

151.   When you finish using a photocopier, reprogram it for 99 copies, 56% reduction, collate, 17 inch paper, extra dark, auto feed, and then make sure to spill correction fluid all over the copy glass.

152.   Pee in swimming pools.

153.   Chew gum.

154.   Carry a big comb or brush in your back pocket.

155.   Tell foreigners that if it weren't for Uncle Sam, they'd all have been slaves in Russian gulags, eating with chopsticks, or speaking German.

156.   Whenever you are visiting friends at their homes, discretely set their alarm clocks to go off at 3:00 a.m.

157.   Pick out a single, unattached male neighbor. Then call the police and scream: "You've got to get over there quick. I think he's beating his wife again."

158.   Enter through "exit" doors, and exit through "enter" doors.

159.   On all applications, list your address as "Unknown."

160.   Walk up to strangers and scream in their faces: "What's your name?"

161. Walk up to strangers and scream in their faces: "Who invited you here?"

162. Tell people that you just got out of prison.

163. Have mementoes dangling from your car's rearview mirror.

164. Eat chili and beans the night before a proctology exam.

165. Let weeds and scrub brush overgrow your lawn.

166. Don't shovel your sidewalks after it snows.

167.   Collect junk in your garage and leave your garage door open.

168.   When you are writing, instead of using dots above *i*'s and *j*'s, draw circles, hearts or stars.

169.   As a gesture of gratitude when staying with friends, always make sure to wash and dry their wool and cashmere clothes.

170.   Shave one side of your head, and paste a postcard to the bald spot.

171.   Put notes on random, dented cars which read: "I'm sorry I bumped into your car. Please call me so that we can make arrangements."

(Make sure to include your phone number on the note.) When people call you, tell them that you are going to sue them.

172.   Wear your watch on your ankle, and check the time constantly.

173.   Tell your employer that you used to be a union organizer.

174.   Buy porno magazines and display them on your coffee table.

175.   Surround your house with barbed wire.

176.   Erect a chain-link fence along the borders of your property.

177.   Become an exotic dancer.

178.   Snore.

179.   Use garlic as a breath freshener.

180.   Ask for a raise.

181.   Wear dirty clothes.

182.   Wear clothes which still have the store tags attached.

183.   Mow your lawn at 6:00 a.m.

184.   Build guard towers on your property, and equip them with searchlights and automatic weapons.

185.   Make "beeping" noises whenever anyone backs up.

186.   While talking with a friend, talk about your "best friend."

187.   Move into a nice neighborhood and then take on boarders.

188.   Turn a rental property into a halfway house.

189.   During conversations start barking like a dog — and don't stop.

190.   Turn up thermostats to maximum cool.

191.   When entertaining vegetarians, serve only veal.

192.   When entertaining serious meat eaters, serve only tofu.

193.   Own a car alarm that constantly gives off false alarms.

194.   Wear curlers in your hair.

195.   Put cold cream on your face before you go to bed.

196.   On job applications, list your hobby as: "Out-of-body travel to The White House and, also, to the bedrooms of people I'm hot for."

197.   Have your home fumigated just before guests arrive.

198.   Turn the ringer volumes to "off" on all phones.

199.   Before you open a pack of cigarettes, "pack" the tobacco (as if that were really necessary) by loudly tapping the pack against your hand, over and over and over again like some kind of freaking nut case.

200.   Tell your brothers and sisters that they are adopted and that you have proof.

201.   Will all of your money to a religious cult.

202.   Have only dial phones in your house.

203.   Spend $1,200.00 on exercise equipment and never use it.

204.   Erect an aluminum/fake Christmas tree.

205.   Drive alone in HOV/car pool lanes.

206.   After treating friends to a nice dinner out, tell them that they are all leaches.

207.   During wedding ceremonies, when the minister says, "If anyone knows any reason why these two people should not be married….," always be sure to stand up and make your opinion heard.

208.   If you're a man, lower the toilet seat before you pee, and raise it after you pee.

209.   Your response to everything anyone says in your presence should always be: "More nonsensical rubbish from the mouths of the

uninformed, undereducated, lower proletariat!"

210.   When you mow your lawn — shave it.

211.   Drive fast over speed bumps.

212.   Specify that your drive-thru orders are "to go."

213.   Scratch your armpits, crotch and rear end in public.

214.   Use loads of cheap hair oil.

215.   Grow a long, waxed mustache.

216.   Tell your neighbors that for the last four nights you've seen a man wearing combat fatigues running around the neighborhood wielding a machete.

217.   During a first appointment with a physician, clearly explain how you have sued your last five doctors for malpractice.

218.   Convert your living room into your "junk room."

219.   Put off romantic advances by saying that you'd rather go jogging.

220.   When you have cash, flash it.

221.   Paint one of your front teeth black.

222.   Grow marijuana on your kitchen windowsill.

223.   If you're a man, shave your armpits.

224.   If you're a woman, quit shaving your armpits.

225.   Buy a pinkie ring and wear it.

226.   Wear two pinkie rings — one on each pinkie.

227.   Have your pets relieve themselves on your neighbor's lawns.

228.   Be late for everything except parties.

229.   Insist that hand dryers replace paper towels in the restrooms where you work.

230.   Stare at people.

231.   Belch, fart and pick your nose — especially during meals.

232.   Fire an employee.

233.   Don't refill ice trays.

234.   Show up for parties an hour early.

235.   Call acquaintances at 2:45 a.m. to chat.

236.   Place a sign on your front door which reads: "Danger — Keep away. Property is contaminated by plutonium, malaria & bubonic plague."

237.   Sit around soaking your fingers in a bowl of Palmolive.   Refer to

everyone as "Madge."

238.   Yawn while listening to other people tell jokes, but laugh uproariously while you tell jokes.

239.   Get a nose ring.

240.   Become a groupie.

241.   Attach a large C. B. radio antennae to your car.

242.   Ask people how much money they make.

243.   Reprimand employees in front of their co-workers, subordinates and customers.

244.   Be pro-choice, but against animal testing.

245.   If the police attempt to pull you over — make a high-speed getaway.

246.   Intentionally drive through puddles so that pedestrians will be splashed.

247.   Mix food together on your plate before you begin eating it.

248.   Spend your free time learning to play country music on a Pan flute.

249. Accuse anyone who does work on your property of having an affair with your husband or wife — even if you aren't married.

250. Tell passengers sitting near you on a loaded plane, train or bus that you have strep throat.

251. List Karl Marx as a reference on job applications.

252. List collection agencies as references on loan applications.

253. Become a pack rat — be obsessive about acquiring too much of everything, and refuse to throw away anything.

254.   When the toilet paper runs out, don't replace it — or put on a new roll backwards.

255.   Grow obsessively long fingernails.

256.   Spend your life accomplishing nothing.

257.   Fall asleep while you are driving.

258.   Smother good steaks with ketchup.

259.   Monopolize conversations.

260. On invitations, spell out all numbers. For example: "The ceremony will be held at four-thirty p.m. on November twenty-third at All Saints Church, Twenty-ten First Street in Santa Idiot's Nest, California."

261. Sign your name with an "X."

262. Always list your year of birth as 1849. If asked about it just say: "There's no mistake. You just don't understand."

263. For special occasions, write with sparkle paint.

264. Shake bottled or canned carbonated beverages before opening them.

265.   Stand up in a busy diner and violently tear a newspaper to shreds while screaming, "It's all lies. It's all lies!"

266.   Take pictures at funerals.

267.   Ask friends to mortgage their homes and lend you $100,000.00.

268.   Describe your bowel movements to people.

269.   Mail warnings to your neighbors to: "Stay off my property!"

270.   Loosen the caps on salt and pepper shakers.

271. Pour oil into your gas tank so that whenever you drive you create a smokescreen.

272. Sincerely confide in people that you are a witch or a warlock and that you can't stop casting spells on people.

273. Change your child's diapers in public.

274. Leave dirty Kleenex in shopping carts.

275. Blow your nose in restaurants.

276.   Wear two different colors and styles of shoes.

277.   After a good meal in a fine restaurant, take out your dentures and wash them in your water glass.

278.   Walk into work wildly waiving your arms and hands back and forth above your head. Continue this behavior throughout the day while creating massive commotion. Explain that it all started the night before and, no matter what you do, you can't stop it. The next day, walk into work and exclaim: "I took an aspirin and it stopped. No big deal!"

279.   Look for, and describe, the worst in everyone.

280.   Use toothpicks in public.

281.   Play tunes by squishing your hands between your soggy armpits.

282.   Make photocopies of your private parts.

283.   Make photocopies of your private parts and mail them to people.

284.   Frame photocopies of your private parts and hang them in your office.

285.   Write letters on lined paper.

286.   Have bread in your left hand while you're eating with your right hand.

287.   Set up a stereo system on your desk. At 10:00 a.m. every morning, jump up and do aerobics to Beethoven's Fifth played at 120 decibles.

288.   Announce that you are running for Mayor. Erect a pup tent in your side yard — make it your campaign headquarters — and demand contributions from your neighbors.

289.   Fall in love with someone who is serving time in prison.

290.   Double park.

291.   Ask fat people if they are pregnant.

292.   Inform your boss that you are quitting to start your own company —
        and that you're going to take all of his customers with you.

293.   Park too close to other cars.

294.   Super-Glue people's things together: books to desks, paper clips to
        keyboards, toothbrushes to sinks, pots and pans to stoves, beer cans to
        refrigerator trays, silverware to plates, plates to tables, etc.

295.   Change the subject during conversations which are important to others.

296.   Try to beat yellow lights.

297.   Every time you see a computer, discreetly turn the light control to dark.

298.   Turn volume controls to maximum on all televisions and radios — regardless of whether they are in operation. Just walk over and do it.

299.   Tell your neighbors that you've discovered your subdivision was built on a toxic waste dump.

300.   Hog the TV remote control.

301.   Pronounce foreign words and terms with foreign accents.

302.   Hide money from your spouse.

303.   Complete only 25% of a hair transplant program. Walk around with a bunch of plugs in your head.

304.   Claim to be "the world's greatest expert" on everything.

305.   Drive a filthy car, full of garbage, with greasy fingerprints smudged all over the windows.

306.   Don't discipline your children.

307.   When pens runs out of ink, don't throw them away. Leave them at the homes of friends or on the desks of co-workers.

308.   At the end of any good meal to which you've been treated, repeatedly stick your finger down your throat — and gag and throw up all over the place. While doing so, angrily accuse the host of trying to poison you.

309.   Steal.

310.   Adjust the flame control to "maximum" on cigarette lighters.

311. Call each of your relatives and tell them that you have listed them as beneficiaries in your will. Two weeks later, call them back and tell them that you've changed your mind.

312. Tell your boyfriend that you're pregnant.

313. Tell your boyfriend that you're pregnant and that he's not the father.

314. Ask your boss for an advance.

315. Take your new love to meet your weird family and friends.

316.   Tell your friends that you've discovered your phone is tapped and that you think theirs might be, too.

317.   Wear sunglasses at night.

318.   Whenever the need arises, pull off your shoes and socks and trim your toenails with your teeth.

319.   Claim that the reason you don't have a checking account is because you don't trust banks: "My bookkeeping and the bank's just never seem to agree. Quite frankly, I don't trust banks, and I have reason not to trust them, and you shouldn't trust them either. If you have about six hours,

I'll explain to you my theory of how the banking system *really* works!"

320.   Test out a friend's new fax machine with stapled pages.

321.   Find time to relax in your deluxe tree house — spying on neighbors through high-powered telescopes.

322.   Whenever someone asks a favor of you, say: "Do you want fries with that?"

323.   Pretend that you are having a heart attack. After someone calls an ambulance, stand up and exclaim: "I am back from the white tunnel."

324. When you write, put periods and commas on the outside of quotation marks. For example: "You write like an idiot", he told me, "and, therefore, you're fired".

325. Cover all of your furniture with sheets.

326. Fall in love with a relative.

327. When cutting down an unwanted tree in your yard, make sure that the tree falls towards your neighbor's house and not yours.

328. Play your stereo loud and with your windows open.

329.   Tell your co-workers that you think they aren't working hard enough and that you're going to talk to the boss about it.

330.   Drive a car with a bent frame that looks like it's going sideways down the road.

331.   Use bad grammar: "Is that them?" "If I was him, I'd prob-ly quit." "I wish it was different."

332.   Use really bad grammar: "Where's Ma gunna park the eighteen wheeler at?" "It don't matter no how." "They come here ex-pecially to see me." "Was you ready to order?" "I done that job beautiful." "He

don't give me nutin." "She axed me, 'Hey, ain't you mah cousin?'"

333.   Build a chapel in a spare bedroom.

334.   Start digging a lake, by hand, in your back yard.

335.   Don't do anything about your dandruff.

336.   Mail to people your thoughts on politics and religion that no one wants
         to read.

337.   Paint big "L's" on the tops of your right shoes, and big "R's" on the

tops of your left shoes. When people comment about it, tell them you're dyslexic."

338.   Give a bottle of mouth wash as a gift.

339.   Become a telephone solicitor.

340.   Tape signs to people's backs which say: "Kick me," or "I'm stupid," etc.

341.   Quit your job without giving a two-week notice.

342.   Don't tell your partner(s) that you have a sexually transmitted disease.

343.   File everything in the wrong places.

344.   Take off sick days from work when you're not sick, and go to work when you are sick.

345.   Don't wash your hands after using the restroom.

346.   Demand that your proper name be used. For example, if your nicknames would be Ben, Benji, Benny or Junior, insist upon being called "Benjamin the Second."

347.   Replace your porch light with a red bulb that blinks on and off.

348.   When visiting friends, plug the drain in their upstairs tub and turn on the water full blast.

349.   Develop an unnatural fear of crossing guards.

350.   Cry wolf.

351.   Overdress or underdress for every event.

352.   Ask someone to help you move.

353.   Ask someone to drive you to, or pick you up from, the airport.

354.   Have hickeys all over your neck.

355.   Page yourself over the office intercom several times per day.

356.   Wear your sideburns too long.

357.   Shave off your sideburns.

358.   Grow a beard.

359.   Constantly proclaim that you are related to royalty.

360.   Go a restaurant, eat a big meal, then claim to have lost your wallet.

361.   Save money by doing your own alterations with a stapler.

362.   Wear too much cologne, perfume or after shave.

363.   Have a long, loud discussion over your cell phone while you're in a public place.

364.   Fly to Hawaii just so you can see your hero, Don Ho.

365.   Call your senator's office from a pay phone and leave this message with his assistant: "Tell the Senator that I finally got the goods on him for that deal of his back in the '80's, and that it's all going to be in the newspapers and on television next week." Then hang up.

366.   Suck your thumb.

367.   Don't own a credit card.

368.   Read newspapers, magazines and books out loud.

369.   Talk to walls.

370.   Live off your mother-in-law.

371.   While approaching a closed door yell: "Open." If the door doesn't open, stand at the door and yell "open" over and over and over until someone opens it. Then say: "It's about time, you incompetent jerk!"

372.   Become a drug addict.

373.   Put on rubber gloves before touching doorknobs.

374.   Carry around your high school yearbook. Offer it for identification when attempting to cash checks or take international flights.

375.   Put a car up on blocks in your driveway.

376.   Store all of your old appliances, tires and empty paint cans in your yard.

377.   Grow a Hitler mustache and change your name to Adolph.

378.   Wear your clothes inside out.

379.   Get special favors from the boss.

380.   Claim that you work for the C. I. A.

381.   Get a tatoo on your face.

382.   Get an ex-lover's name tattooed onto your rear end.

383.   Become grossly obese.

384.   Own only a black and white television set.

385.   When you wear a tie, make sure that the short end is in front.

386.   Run out of an optometrists's office screaming: "He blinded me! He blinded me!"

387. Put your wastebasket on top of your desk. Label it "IN."

388. Refer to your stereo system as a "Victrola."

389. Carry a gun and a fake police badge wherever you go. Display them often while introducing yourself as "Officer Dinko."

390. Take your dog to work with you until it's house-trained.

391. Make extra money by holding a continuous garage sale.

392. Set back the time on all clocks by twenty-seven minutes.

393.   Don't keep life preservers in your boat.

394.   Sculpture your chest hair.

395.   Favor one child over another.

396.   Allow white stuff to collect on the corners of your mouth.

397.   Create an uncontrollable computer virus.

398.   Don't pay your bills.

399. Build an elaborate, lighted Christmas display outside your home on Memorial Day.

400. Wear a business suit to a rock concert.

401. Serve caffeinated coffee and soft drinks to people who suffer from panic attacks.

402. Invite your adult relatives, but not their children, to family events.

403. Whenever you meet a person from another country, start conversing in any foreign language you know.

404. Pull up to a bank drive-thru window and ask for a cheeseburger and fries.

405. Tell your boss that he or she's an idiot.

406. Hold a fake funeral for yourself.

407. Walk up to someone at a party and say: "No one likes you."

408. When traveling through the South, always refer to the locals as "crackers."

409. Bathe your dog in the kitchen sink.

410. Sell someone a car that you know is going to blow up any minute.

411. Become a counterfeiter.

412. Put lawn ornaments all over your property.

413. Ask your neighbors if you can come over and preach to them.

414. Understate your weight.

415. Overstate your height.

416. Use permanent markers on grease boards.

417. Unload a full shopping cart of groceries at the "express lane."

418. Let your teeth rot.

419. File for divorce.

420. Leave long, rambling messages on answering machines and voice mails.

421.   Make all telephone calls to overseas numbers from your friend's telephones.

422.   Leave less than a 15% tip.

423.   Individually ask people at your class reunion about their occupations. Upon hearing each answer say: "Oh, I am sorry. It sounds like you're a complete failure. Now let me tell you about my fab-u-lous life!"

424.   Write hate mail.

425.   Win the lottery.

426.   Become a swinger.

427.   Talk too much.

428.   Reveal secrets.

429.   Tell employees that you're going to send them to an all-expenses-paid convention in New York. Then hand them bus tickets.

430.   Visit an old girlfriend and her husband, or visit an old boyfriend and his wife.

431. Become a gambling addict.

432. Tear out the ceramic tile and hardwood floors from your house and install linoleum and wall-to-wall carpeting.

433. At the height of a party, stop the music and tell everyone that they have to leave.

434. Use a metal spatula to scrape off the ice from a friend's windshield.

435. Repeat the alphabet in reverse, out loud, over and over.

436.   Go AWOL the day after becoming a scout troop leader.

437.   Accidentally drop hot cigarette ashes on someone else's furniture.

438.   Begin each letter you write with "I..."

439.   Invent a time machine and don't let anyone else use it.

440.   Commit suicide.

441.   Liquidate everything and put all of your money into the commodities market.

442.   Stand around talking to yourself.

443.   Pop your zits in public.

444.   Ask people to pop your zits for you.

445.   Ask people if you can pop their zits for them.

446.   Spend eleven years locked in your basement looking for "the answer."

447.   Hang pictures of yourself throughout your house.

448.   Become a lawyer.

449.   Don't heat or clean your swimming pool.

450.   Move back to your hometown and ruin your family's reputation.

451.   Buy pet tarantulas and snakes. Let them wonder freely around your home.

452.   Get a dog that barks constantly, and keep it outside.

453.   Constantly send e-mail and fax blasts to your bosses and co-workers

informing them of every important move you make. For example: "Just wanted to let you know that, today, I parked near a tree!"

454.   Blame everything you do wrong on others.

455.   Frequently send to your relatives letters in sealed envelopes marked: "Don't open until I'm dead!"

456.   Buy a drum set for your apartment.

457.   Join the K. K. K.

458.   Max out your credit cards and then file bankruptcy.

459.   Wait until your parents have raised you and put you through college —
        then disown them.

460.   Call the wrong number ten times in a row.

461.   Spike a friend's drink with LSD.

462.   The day before your closing date on a new house, leave on a European
        vacation.

463.   Break down and start crying about your problems during a celebration.

464.   Begin every sentence with, "Hey Dude,...."

465.   Hire a private detective to investigate your family, co-workers and friends. Upon completion, send to them the findings.

466.   Marry someone of a different race.

467.   Wear your underwear on the outside of your clothes.

468.   Carry a three-inch thick wallet, full of unnecessary cards, receipts and

pictures, in your back pocket.

469.   Don't tell your betrothed, who dreams of having children with you, that you've had your teeth capped, a nose job, sandblasting, a chin implant, liposuction, and that you wear tinted contacts and a hair weave.

470.   Use your family's rent money to go to a NASCAR race.

471.   Hold nightly seances.

472.   Whenever you see a properly programmed VCR, immediately press the reset button.

473.   Forget holidays, birthdays and anniversaries.

474.   Become a hermit.

475.   Talk to your invisible friends.

476.   If you're a doctor, tell people that "nutritional supplements are a bunch of nonsense."

477.   Use big words you can't pronounce or that you don't understand.

478.   Buy a mail order degree — and then use it as if it were real.

479.   Join an outlaw motorcycle gang and invite them to your house for Sunday picnics.

480.   Use products which turn your toilet water blue.

481.   Become a voyeur — a peeping Tom.

482.   Pretend you don't recognize your friends and family. Pretend you've never heard of them.

483.   Allow pets to eat food from your plate.

484.   Decorate your computer monitor with pins, buttons, stamps and bumper stickers.

485.   Wear pajamas to work, to the supermarket — wherever you go.

486.   If you're a man, grow a ponytail.

487.   Change lanes without using your turn signal.

488.   Spread rumors.

489.   Dress your dog in clothes.

490.   Run out of gas on a busy thoroughfare.

491.   Don't show up for a date.

492.   Press *69 on your phone after you receive a hang-up call.

493.   Give a beautifully wrapped, empty box as a present.

494.   Stick a straw into your nose and drink fluids through it.

495.   Chew your nails and then spit the clippings at people.

496.   Don't iron your clothes.

497.   Button your buttons through the wrong holes.

498.   Get on top of your refrigerator and squat down. When people walk into the kitchen — jump off and scare the hell out of them.

499.   Spill soft drinks into someone's audio tape, video tape or CD collection.

500.   Affix stamps to envelopes sideways.

501.   Throw snowballs at cars.

502.   Delete phone numbers from telephone speed dial memories. Then program in the phone numbers of 900# phone sex companies, the Prime Minister of Norway, the Federal Bureau of Investigation's Organized Crime Hotline, etc.

503.   Every time you take a sip of a liquid — gargle it.

504.   Put fish, worms, frogs and leftover meals into bottled water coolers.

505.   "Read" newspapers, magazines and books upside down.

506.   Live like a king or queen until you go broke. Then live off family and friends.

507.   Smoke someone's last cigarette.

508.   Call collect.

509.   Surround yourself with idiots.

510.   When someone asks: "How are you?" — explain to them the grizzly truth in detail.

511.   Lick your thumb or fingers before you count money, turn pages, etc.

512.   Go skinny dipping in a public pool.

513.   Constantly remind people that you graduated from grade school.

514.   Change your first name often, use different first names, and always select names to use which have substance, such as: Face, Yveondaella, Abra Cadabra or Chachi.

515.   If you're a woman, quit shaving your legs.

516.   If you're a man, wear panty hose.

517.   If you're a Mediterranean woman, grow a mustache.

518.   Talk extra loudly.

519.   Get a dog which bites people.

520.   Be a hypocrite.

521.   Don't vacuum your carpets or rugs.

522. Tell your minister that you are converting to Catholicism.

523. Inform your rabbi that you are converting to Islam.

524. Have more children to increase the amount of your welfare check.

525. Decide that you're an artist and practice your artwork on random appliances, furniture, walls and carpets.

526. Whenever you are introduced to people, ask them for identification.

527. Watch professional wrestling and argue that it's real.

528.   Write bad checks.

529.   Follow a person around for hours.

530.   Move into your car and park it in front of Mr. and Mrs. Someone's house. Whenever the need arises, ask Mr. and Mrs. Someone if you may use their bathroom. Don't be bashful about asking for clean towels, shampoo, and something to eat while you're at it.

531.   Shoot rubber bands at people.

532.   Run into a business, say there's an emergency and that you need to use

their telephone. Then call Dominoes and order a pizza.

533.   Move to a new town and tell all the natives how badly it "sucks."

534.   File sexual harassment charges against your co-workers.

535.   Talk during TV programs, but be silent during commercials.

536.   Get an unlisted telephone number.

537.   Become anorexic.

538.	Claim that all good ideas were yours.

539.	Move in with your children.

540.	Join the mob.

541.	Drool.

542.	Install security cameras in your home.

543.	Wear long, shinny, ventless, cuffless, padded, used Italian suits with unalterable back-roll, collar-gap, and lapel-bulges — without a shirt.

544.   Smoke two cigarettes at a time.

545.   Quit wearing deodorant.

546.   Insist that you were abducted by a U. F. O.

547.   Build a U. F. O. landing strip in your back yard.

548.   Become a model rocketry hobbyist, and conduct daily launches from your roof or through your bedroom windows.

549.   Wear a winter coat and goulashes in the summertime.

550.   Take a "dump" in someone's pool.

551.   Allow your negligence and incompetence to hold back the progress of others.

552.   Talk people into making bad investments.

553.   Become obsessed with conspiracies.

554.   Don't pay your child support.

555.   Eat all of the donuts at work.

556.   If you're a grown man, pierce your ear(s).

557.   Drive with an expired driver's license.

558.   Drive with expired license plates.

559.   Drive while you're under the influence of alcohol or drugs.

560.   Cancel your engagement but keep the shower gifts.

561.   Sponsor someone into a multi level marketing deal, make them buy a bunch of products, and then disappear.

562.   Wear polyester.

563.   Ride a bicycle on a busy street.

564.   During telephone conversations, put people "on hold" — and leave them there.

565.   Write using phonetic spelling.

566.   Wear tinted eyeglasses.

567.   Have diamonds imbedded in your front teeth.

568.   Tape an electric alarm clock to your wrist, and plug yourself in whenever you need to know the time.

569.   Tell people how cool you are.

570.   For Thanksgiving dinner, serve Sloppy Joe's on stale buns.

571.   Become a door-to-door salesman.

572.   When correcting your children in public, always speak loud enough to impress everyone in the area with your wisdom.

573.   Borrow a friend's car — and burn rubber as you drive away.

574.   Quit your job and move to Tahiti.

575.   Leave your home wearing nothing but old boxer shorts and a football helmet.

576.   Park on a busy bridge and fish out of your car window.

577.   Use someone else's toothbrush.

578.   Whenever someone swears, fall to your knees and start praying.

579.   Spend hours trying to eat a steak with a spoon.

580.   Wear a wig.

581.   Kindly ask someone to save your place in a line — then disappear.

582.   Take a two-week vacation in England — and come back with a British accent.

583.   Leave your children with a friend "for a few minutes" so that you can "run to the store." Then go to a bar and get drunk.

584.   Mimic a person's every move.

585.   Speak in Pig Latin.

586.   Wear kids-colored bandages.

587.   Have your neck shortened.

588.   See how long your nose hairs will grow.

589.   Win a power struggle at work, accept the resulting promotion — then resign.

590.   Drain your swimming pool and use it as a garbage dump.

591.   Order a delivery and then leave the house.

592.   Wait until you are fifty years old to get braces.

593.   Become a bounty hunter.

594.   Wear a name tag 24-hours per day.

595.   Fart in a crowded elevator — then hit the "Emergency Stop" button.

596.   Borrow things from people — and never return them.

597.   Whenever you see anyone alone, walk up to them and scream: "Don't you have *any* friends?"

598.   Litter.

599.   Wear old-style, lined bifocals.

600.   Put decaffeinated coffee in the office coffee maker for a month. After everyone has overcome their caffeine addictions, switch to Moroccan espresso.

601.   Park your car in spaces reserved for other people.

602.   Disappear.

603.   Lie.

604.   Collect all the trash from your car and stuff it into the transaction box at a bank drive-thru window. Ask the teller: "Say, could you take care of this for me? Thanks. Bye, Bye."

605.   Always have a good excuse for being late: "Bill Gates and I were cruising at Mach 1.2 while discussing quantum mechanics. Suddenly,

our plane was attacked by elements of the North Korean Air Force — and we had to bailout over Rio. Otherwise, I would have been here."

606.   Carry your lunch in an old dog food bag.

607.   Run a singles ad in the newspaper. When people respond, tell them you just got out of a mental institution.

608.   Hand out business cards which state that you are a gynecologist and that you offer free exams.

609.   Carry on your shoulder a big, 200-watt per channel boom box/ghetto

blaster. Crank it up, and take it with you everywhere: to the country club, the doctor's office, business meetings, P. T. A. meetings, etc.

610. Write in handwriting so bad that no one can read what you've written.

611. Enjoy a box of popcorn and a Coke while you're at the symphony.

612. Lose someone else's keys.

613. Frequently telephone your parents during your honeymoon.

614. Pluck-out your eyelashes, shave off your eyebrows, shave your head

and your body, and dye your skin blue. Tell people you're an alien here to conquer earth.

615. Simultaneously extend your index and pinkie fingers to point at people, places or things.

616. Blow your nose in the shower.

617. Walk around with an attache case upon which there is a sign that reads: "Live Ebola Virus Samples."

618. Snap bra straps.

619.   Kidnap yourself, collect the ransom money donated by friends and family, then hold a welcome home party for yourself in your new mansion.

620.   Drive slowly in passing lanes.

621.   Ask friends, co-workers and family if you can borrow their credit cards.

622.   Loosely tie the calves of your legs together with a rope and waddle around. Tell people it's deprivation therapy.

623.   Eat oatmeal, cereal, eggs, soup, etc., with your hands.

624.   Walk around with your fly open.

625.   Live in a slum but drive a luxury car.

626.   Pay for potato chips and pop with food stamps.

627.   Marry a foreigner and move overseas. During visits home, complain about how bad the United States is.

628.   Put a cuckoo clock in a guestroom.

629.   Wear brown shoes to a formal event.

630.   At the end of passionate love making, either immediately fall asleep or get dressed and leave.

631.   Never send "Thank You" cards.

632.   Sit in the middle of your yard shooting at birds.

633.   Don't return phone calls.

634.   Wear glasses with dirty, oily, scratched lenses.

635.   Turn all the pictures and the televisions in your house upside down.

636.   Ride a motorcycle without a helmet.

637.   Put a sign on your front door which reads: "You are not wanted here. Go away."

638.   Install strobe lights in your bathrooms.

639.   Save money by killing your meals — whether it be deer, 'possum, racoon, etc. Mail samples of these culinary treats to your friends, and make underwear out of the remaining fur.

640. If you have a glass eye, take it out and tap it on your desk while you're thinking.

641. Leave ash trays full of cigarette butts.

642. Have other people do your dirty work for you.

643. Put hot pots and pans into cold water.

644. Share intimate pictures of past loves.

645. Move without leaving a forwarding address.

646. Hopscotch, limp, skip, shuffle, crawl, high step, goose step, swagger, trot or prance — instead of walking normally.

647. Take advantage of intellectual inferiors.

648. Get arrested.

649. Use profanity.

650. Have temper tantrums.

651. Don't take care of your health.

652.   Be unappreciative.

653.   Come out of the closet.

654.   Wear a puppet on your hand which does your talking for you.

655.   Refer to your car, van or truck as a "vehicle."

656.   Refer to a person as an "individual," and to people as "individuals."

657.   Wear your pants backwards.

658. Don't stand up when a woman enters the room.

659. Play mind games.

660. When someone asks for directions, send them to Timbuktu.

661. Suffer from pimples and black heads and don't do anything about it.

662. Stand behind people while they are being interviewed on TV. Jump, wave, scream, make stupid faces, and say, "Hi," to your mamma.

663. Be stubborn.

664.   Frown.

665.   Live in the past.

666.   Talk out loud in theaters.

667.   If you're a woman, wear too much jewelry.

668.   If you're a man, wear any jewelry.

669.   Dig foxholes in your yard.

670.   Rip people off.

671.   Fall for someone of a lower class.

672.   Don't file tax returns.

673.   Immediately after picking up a woman for a first date, tell her that you have to stop at a drug store and get some condoms. Ask her if she prefers "ribbed" or "smooth."

674.   Immediately after leaving on a first date with a man, tell him that you need to stop at a drug store to get something for your "terrible yeast

infection."

675.   Serve burned toast.

676.   Have dirty fingernails.

677.   Fly the flag of another country in your yard.

678.   Commit an insurance scam.

679.   Be a hypochondriac.

680.   Become addicted to porno sites on the Internet.

681.   Carry around pictures of Ozzie and Harriet Nelson. Insist that they are your "real" parents.

682.   Buy gaudy accessories for your car.

683.   Wear your tie "L. A. style."

684.   Put continuous strings of blinking lights on your Christmas tree.

685.   Get a "shag" haircut.

686.   Smoke nonfiltered cigarettes.

687.   Burn bridges.

688.   Talk before you think.

689.   Play "chicken" with other cars.

690.   Kick people while they're down.

691.   Drive with your windshield wipers on in perfect weather.

692.   Continue a long-term relationship but refuse to make a commitment.

693.   Play darts in a crowded room.

694.   Become a transvestite.

695.   Drop by someone's house without calling first.

696.   Fail to vote.

697.   If you wear a hearing aid, keep the volume turned too low, and constantly yell at people: "WHAT DID YOU SAY?"

698.   Drive around town on a riding lawnmower.

699.   Park in Handicapped Parking spaces without a permit.

700.   Insist upon paying for things with I. O. U.'s

701.   Buy more than one lottery ticket at a time.

702.   Fail to complete tasks.

703.   During a conversation, start speaking in a foreign language. Then say, "Oh, I'm sorry; for a moment there I forgot which country I was in."

704.   Become a religious fanatic.

705.   Hold a loud party in a small motel room.

706.   Talk negatively.

707.   Wear a tie chain.

708.   Spend the family's fortune.

709.   Demand that your friends and relatives be cremated.

710.   Gain weight after you get married.

711.   Lose weight after you get divorced.

712.   Be unappreciative.

713.   Take up more than one space when you park.

714.   Don't carry proper car, health, home, or life insurance.

715.   Whenever you borrow a pen or pencil, immediately, and in full view
        of the lender, begin chewing on it — then clean your ears with it.

716.   Elope.

717.   Drive in reverse/backwards through bank or restaurant drive-thru's.

718.   Give someone a bad reference.

719.   Maintain a secure, climate-controlled exhibit of unicorn statuettes.

720.   Wear pants that are too long or too short, and blouses/shirts with sleeves that are too long or too short, and collars that are too big.

721.   Clone yourself.

722.   Don't get treatment for mental disorders.

723.   Flip-the-bird at people.

724.   Arrive at work late and leave early.

725.   Blow bubbles with your saliva.

726.   Become an Elvis impersonator.

727.   When you're a guest at a party, always point out what you would have done to make it better.

728.   Be a bully.

729.   Marry for money.

730.   Run out of treats on Halloween.

731.   Get turned on during a therapeutic massage.

732.   Don't show up for reunions.

733.   Spend several days and nights in a row watching cartoons on television.

734.   Name your private parts and talk to them often.

735.   Play Russian roulette.

736.   Play Russian roulette with an automatic pistol.

737.   Have major surgery based upon the opinion of just one doctor.

738.   Call your significant other's ex- for advice.

739.   Fill expensive bottles with cheap liquor.

740.   Play golf or bathe during lightning storms.

741.   Forge someone's name on a document.

742.   Own a sprinkler system that wets pedestrians on the sidewalk and spots up cars as they pass on the street.

743.   Dye the fur on your dog or cat.

744.   Tuck your pant legs into your cowboy boots.

745.   Rush someone who is using the bathroom.

746.   Fall asleep during important events.

747.   Drive a big, fancy pick up truck that will never see a dirt road.

748.   Claim to be a friend of celebrities you've never met.

749.   After you move a chess piece, suddenly scream: "Wait. I changed my mind." Then move the piece to a different square.

750.   Take people for a boat ride on the Niagra River — and run out of gas.

The End